FARM EXPLORER

Why Do Pigs Like Mud?

QUESTIONS AND ANSWERS ABOUT FARM ANIMALS

by Katherine Rawson

CAPSTONE PRESS
a capstone imprint

Published by Pebble Sprout, an imprint of Capstone.

1710 Roe Crest Drive, North Mankato, Minnesota 56003

capstonepub.com

Library of Congress Cataloging-in-Publication Data

Names: Rawson, Katherine, author.

Title: Why do pigs like mud? : questions and answers about farm animals / by Katherine Rawson.

Description: North Mankato, Minnesota : Pebble, [2022] | Series: Farm explorer | Audience: Ages 5-8 | Audience: Grades K-1 | Summary: "Pigs, cows, chickens, and horses—farms have lots of animals! Where do they live? What do they eat? Kids can find answers to all their questions about farm animals in this interactive Pebble Sprout series"—Provided by publisher.

Identifiers: LCCN 2021970051 (print) | LCCN 2021970052 (ebook) | ISBN 9781666349184 (hardcover) | ISBN 9781666349221 (paperback) | ISBN 9781666349269 (pdf) | ISBN 9781666349344 (kindle edition)

Subjects: LCSH: Livestock—Juvenile literature. | Farms—Juvenile literature.

Classification: LCC SF75.5 .R38 2022 (print) | LCC SF75.5 (ebook) | DDC 636—dc23/eng/20220111

LC record available at https://lccn.loc.gov/2021970051

LC ebook record available at https://lccn.loc.gov/2021970052

Editorial Credits:

Editor: Kristen Mohn; Designer: Sarah Bennett; Media Researcher: Julie De Adder; Production Specialist: Katy LaVigne

Image Credits:

Associated Press: Omaha World-Herald/Sarah Hoffman, 23 (top); Getty Images: BushAlex, cover (pig), dageldog, 20 (top), EyeEm/Elise King, 26, Fug4s, 24 (top), shorrocks, 28 (left); Shutterstock: 06photo, 6 (bottom), Alexander Raths, 17, Alexey Kuznetsov, 21 (back), Anneka, 29, Anthony Paz, 19 (bed), bestv, 8 (bottom), Buravleva stock, cover (bathtub), c1sa, 30, Chatuphon Nachanta, 11, Cheryl Ann Quigley, 22, Coatesy, cover (bottom left), Danny Smythe, 13 (tub), DG-Studio, 18 (scale), Dimedrol68, 11 (clock), DominikPhoto, 15, Edoma, 21 (horse), Ekaterina V. Borisova, 12, Eric Isselee, 3, 8 (top), 18 (left), Ewa Studio, 31 (bottom left), Fotoeventis, 16 (top), Four Oaks, 32 (bottom left), Inesmeierfotografie, 31 (bottom right), jack_photo, 7, Jason Grant, cover (pasture), Jeka, 23 (bottom), kurt, 5 (cow), LightField Studios, 19 (blanket), Litvalifa, 4, maljuk, 28 (right), mariusgabi, 6 (top), Martin Bergsma, 27 (mustache and beard), Max_555, 10, Mega Pixel, 25 (poster), Mikhail Malyshev, 6 (middle), Nataliia Pyzhova, 24 (bottom), Nick Beer, 13 (back), Nina Plotitsyna, 19 (foal), 20 (bottom), Olga Pasynkova (background), back cover and throughout, Peter Cripps, 14, photomaster, 27 (turkey), 31 (top), 32 (bottom right), Robert Wolkaniec, 5 (back), Roi and Roi, cover (mud in bathtub), RS 74, cover (bottom middle), SakSa, 25 (back), Sophie Mahdavi, 32 (top), stockphoto mania, 13 (chicken taking bath), SviatlanaLaza, 21 (sneakers), taviphoto, 18 (right), Vector Tradition, 16 (bottom), WDnet Creation, cover (bottom right), yaibuabann, 9

moo! Oink! Baaaaaaaa!

All kinds of animals live on farms. They make food and other products for people to use. Farmers have to take good care of their animals.

Let's find out about farm animals!

Read each question and try to guess the answer. Then turn the page to learn the answer.

Did you guess right?

What do cows have for dinner?

Baby calves
drink milk,
of course.

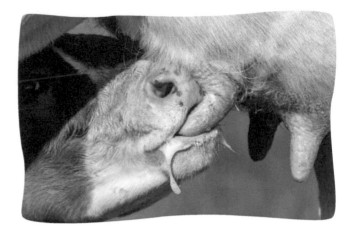

Adult cows eat
hay, grain, and
leftovers from food
processing, such as
soy meal made from
soybean plants.

Cows in a
pasture also
eat lots of
fresh grass.

How much milk does
a cow make every day?

Some kinds of cows produce more milk than others. Black-and-white Holstein cows are the top milk makers.

They can produce about 9 gallons (34 liters) of milk every day!

Do ducks lay eggs that you can eat?

Yes, they do, and you can eat them the same ways you eat chicken eggs—scrambled, fried, or boiled!

Duck eggs are larger than chicken eggs, and they have a stronger flavor.

Do roosters only crow at dawn?

Roosters can crow any time of day.

They crow to claim their territory, to warn the flock of danger, or just to say, "Here I am!"

I'm the boss here!

Do chickens take baths?

Yes, they do! But they don't use soap and water.

Chickens take dust baths by rolling on the ground and covering their feathers with dust. The dust helps keep their feathers dry and clean.

Why do pigs like mud?

Chickens like dust, but pigs LOVE mud.

Mud is cool and wet. Since pigs don't sweat, rolling around in mud is one way they can keep cool.

 It also keeps bugs from biting them!

What's the difference
between a pig and a hog?

A pig and a hog are the same animal, but a hog is one that weighs at least 120 pounds (54 kilograms).

So a hog is really just a big pig.

Horses often nap while standing. That way, if a predator comes near, the horse can quickly run away.

When horses need a deep sleep, they lie down.

How fast can a horse run?

The average speed of a horse at full gallop is around 25 to 30 miles (40 to 48 kilometers) per hour. That's faster than most bicycles!

Race horses can reach speeds of 40 miles (64 km) per hour or more!

How many sweaters
can you get from one sheep?

It depends on how woolly the sheep is!

One sheep can produce 2 to 30 pounds
(0.9 to 13.6 kg) of wool each year.

A sweater weighs about
a pound, so that's up
to 30 sweaters
per sheep.

What is a llama's job on a farm?

LLAMA FOR HIRE

A llama's job is to guard sheep. It protects the flock by scaring away predators or by herding the sheep toward a safer place.

Do turkeys have beards?

Male turkeys have a tuft of black, hairlike feathers called a beard, but it grows from the chest, not the chin.

turkey beard

The older the turkey is, the longer the beard grows.

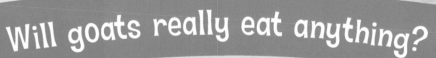

Will goats really eat anything?

Goats are actually quite picky about what they eat. They do eat things that other animals might not, including thorny rose bushes and even poison ivy.

 But they won't eat cans and bottles!

Fun Farm Facts!

Pigs have poor eyesight. However, they have very good hearing as well as a good sense of smell.

A milking cow eats between 50 and 100 pounds (23-45 kg) of food and drinks 30 to 50 gallons (114-189 L) of water a day. Cows need lots of food and water to produce milk!

Horses have a special way of locking the joints in their legs. This keeps them from falling down when they nap while standing.

Most sheep that are raised for their wool have white wool because white can be dyed any color. However, some sheep have wool that is naturally colored. It can be brown, black, gray, or red.

Goats, sheep, and cows don't have upper front teeth. Instead they have a hard pad. That, together with their lower front teeth, are all they need for tearing off the plants they eat.

Turkeys are known for the gobbling sound they make, but only male turkeys gobble. Females chirp and cluck.